LITTLE MONSTER
AROUND the WORLD

Little Monster Travels the World

What a mess! Where are we?

It looks just like a bed...cave! The bed-cave of a very curious young monster. There he is. He's playing video games—his favorite! He also loves books, toy trains, and maps.

Little Monster never wants to go to bed!
Every night, he opens his atlas and closely studies the continents.
And the deserts and mountains. Earth is really big!

His mom decides they're going to go on an adventure. If Little Monster won't sleep, they might as well have fun!

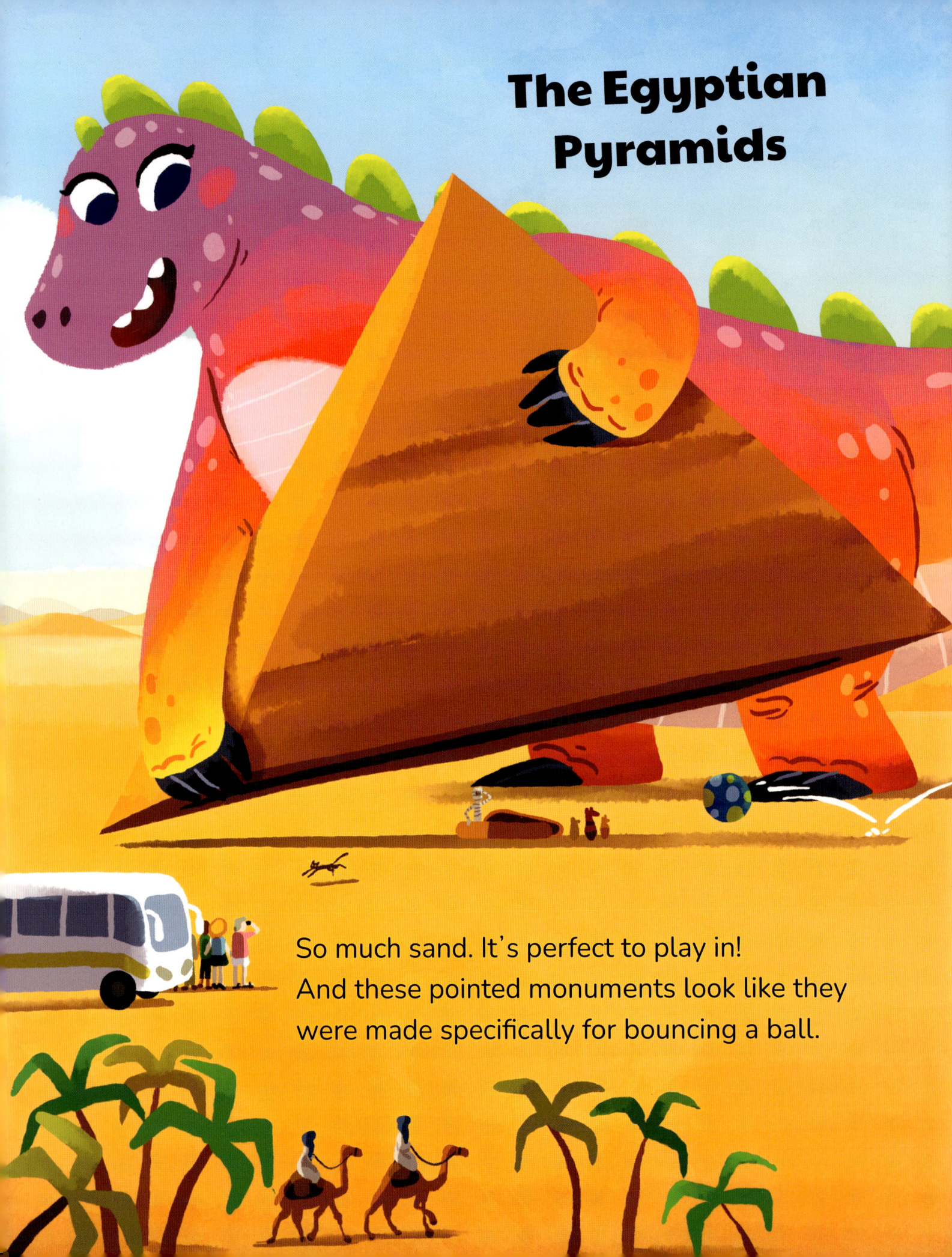

The Egyptian Pyramids

So much sand. It's perfect to play in! And these pointed monuments look like they were made specifically for bouncing a ball.

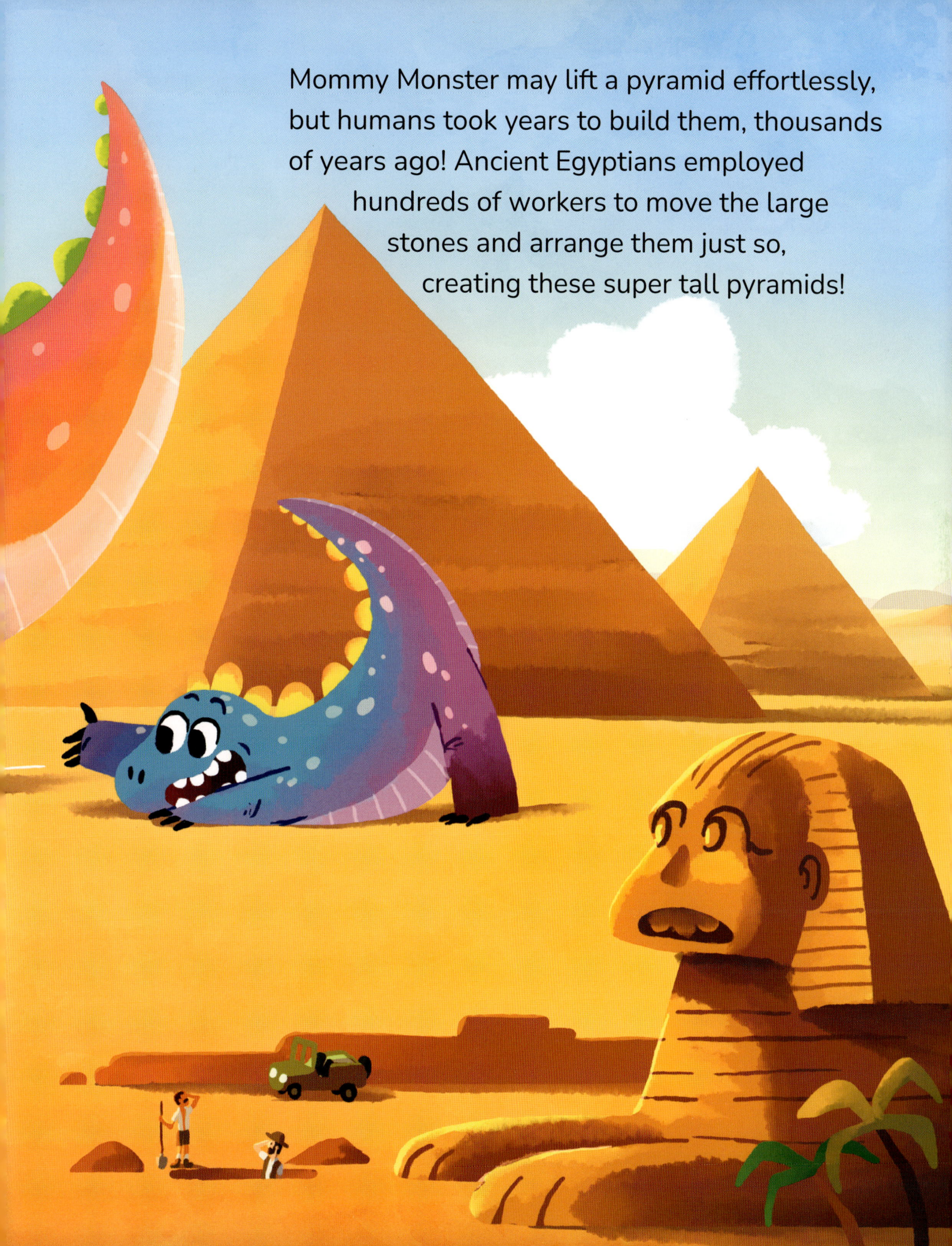
Mommy Monster may lift a pyramid effortlessly, but humans took years to build them, thousands of years ago! Ancient Egyptians employed hundreds of workers to move the large stones and arrange them just so, creating these super tall pyramids!

Little Monster slides down the slopes of the highest mountain in the world! This cold, pure white snow is called "perennial snow." It's so cold here that the snow never melts, lasting year after year. It's the perfect place to have fun with a toboggan if you're a little monster looking for adventure!

Little Monster is balancing on top of a very tall building that looks like it's touching the sky. Or better yet, tickling it! That's why many people call it by a very funny name: "skyscraper."

This large city is home to dozens of skyscrapers, inside which super-fast elevators transport people up and down.

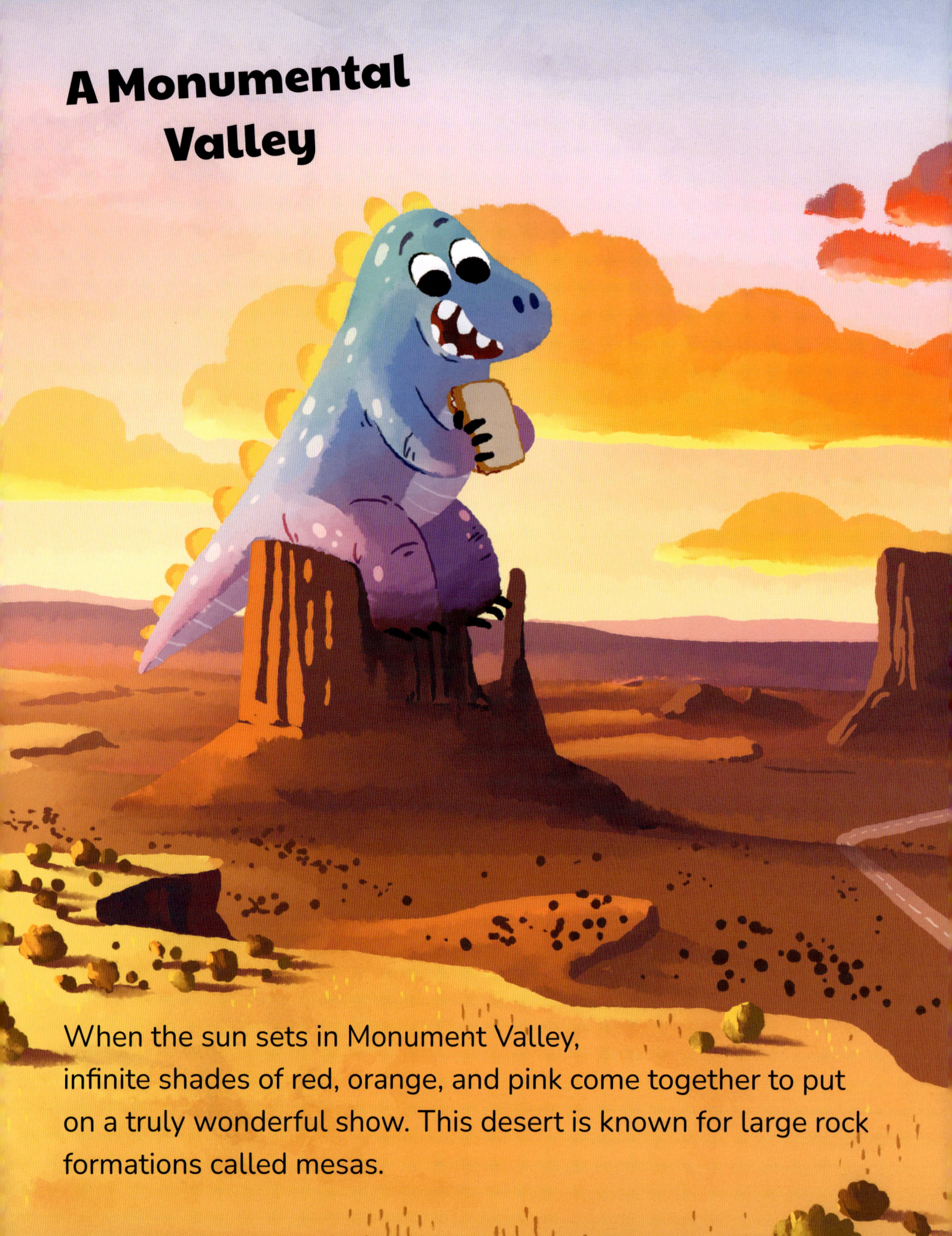

A Monumental Valley

When the sun sets in Monument Valley, infinite shades of red, orange, and pink come together to put on a truly wonderful show. This desert is known for large rock formations called mesas.

They're perfect for a picnic, aren't they, Little Monster?

The Amazon Rainforest

Watch where you step, little one!

Here the vegetation is so dense that it's hard to find a place to walk. This amazing forest is home to thousands of different plants and animals!

And what's that thing that looks like a snake?
The Amazon River, the longest river in the world!

Mount Fuji

Little Monster takes a bath in a calm lake in Japan. But what's that on the horizon? Japan's highest mountain, Fuji!

Do you want to know a secret, Little Monster?
There are three active volcanoes on that mountain.
That means they could erupt at any time!

Out and About on the Great Wall

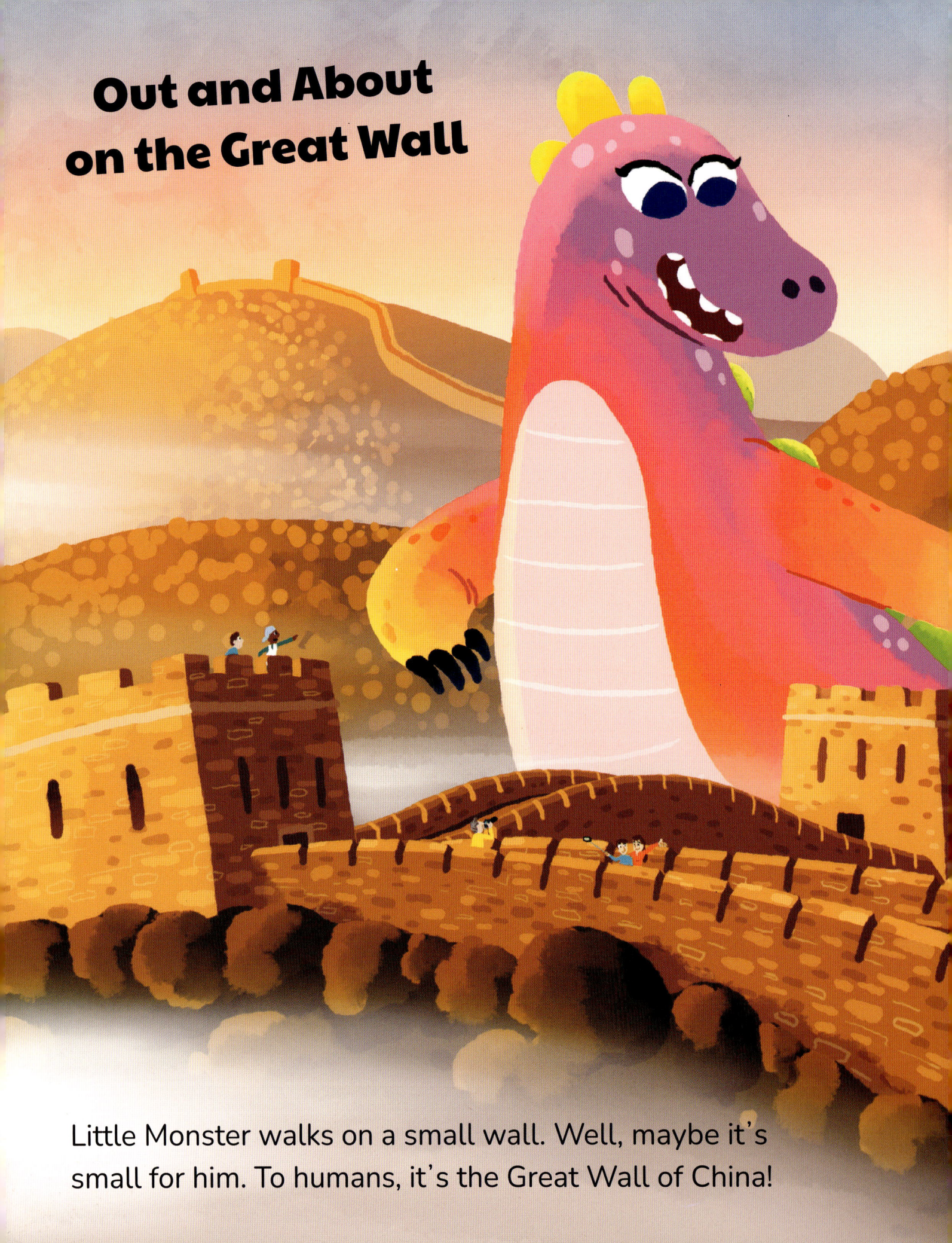

Little Monster walks on a small wall. Well, maybe it's small for him. To humans, it's the Great Wall of China!

It's the biggest, grandest thing ever built. It's very, very long and took many years to build. To cover it all, you'd have to walk for months and months! But not Little Monster. He hops easily along it!

Amid Ice and Penguins

Little Monster and his mom are in Antarctica, near the South Pole. What's that? A floating ice island? That's right! Except it's called an "iceberg," and it's a huge chunk of ice that is drifting out at sea!

This, on the other hand, is a penguin colony! The emperor penguin is an animal species that lives in Antarctica. Penguins are cute, aren't they?

In Australia

Little Monster, you're very good at jumping!
Playing with kangaroos must be so much fun.

Did you know that these wonderful animals are found only here in Australia? They can jump very high and move really fast. And they're marsupials because the females carry their young in a pouch on their belly.

In Rome

No, Little Monster, that isn't a bathtub!
That monument is called the Colosseum, and thousands of years ago it was used as a theater. It's where ancient Romans used to go to see exciting competitions.

Though Little Monster almost got it right! Sometimes it was filled with water and small boats sailed within it, pretending to engage in naval battles, called *naumachias*.

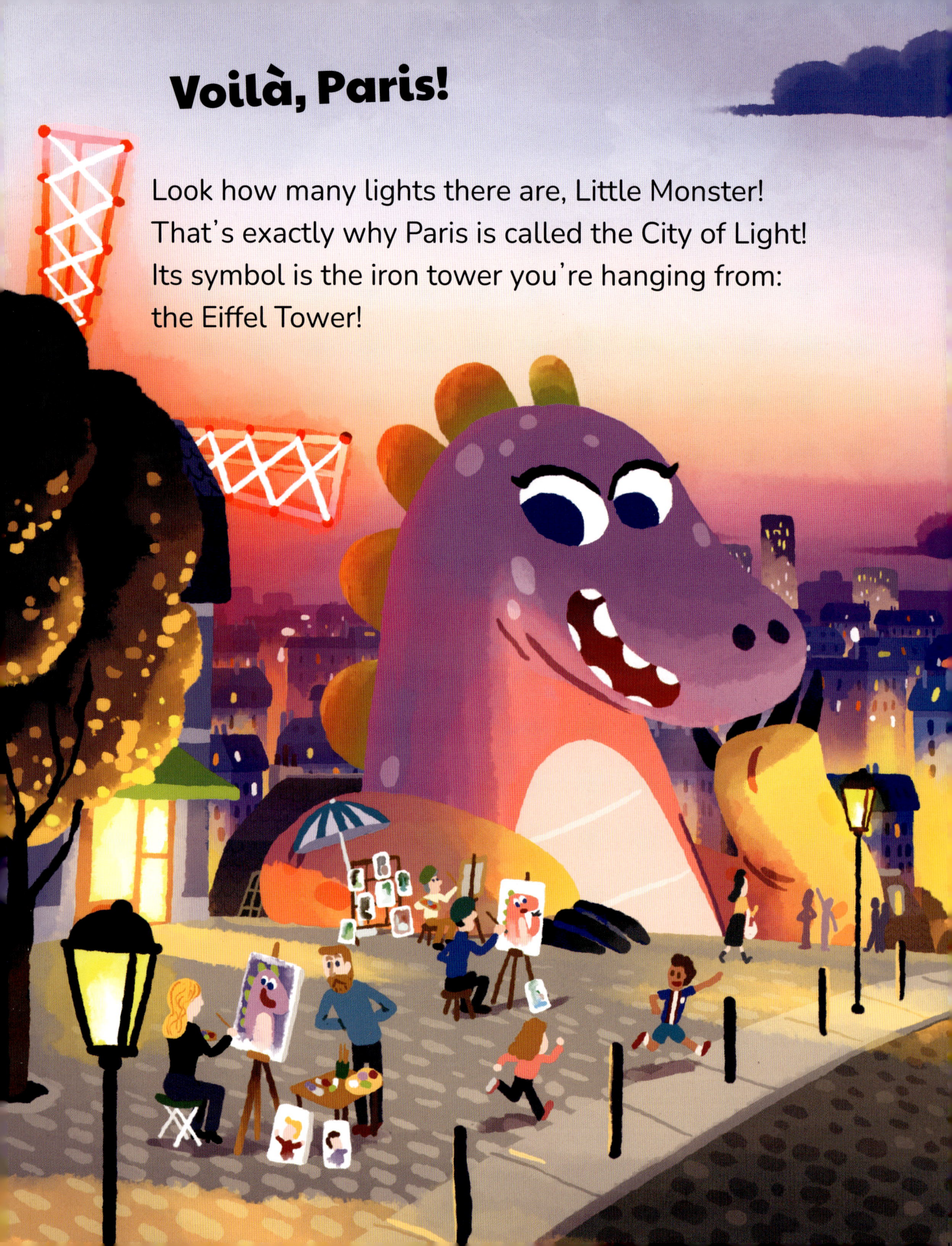

Voilà, Paris!

Look how many lights there are, Little Monster! That's exactly why Paris is called the City of Light! Its symbol is the iron tower you're hanging from: the Eiffel Tower!

There are hundreds of steps that lead up to the top, but don't worry, there are fast elevators, too!

London

Hey, Little Monster, that double-decker bus isn't a toy!
It transports people far and wide in this metropolis.
Put it down, and listen. Big Ben is playing!

What is it?

It's a large bell in a clock tower. Its chimes echo through the heart of the city and over the River Thames.

Little Monster and his mother visited so many wonderful places! Can you find them on the map?

CONCEPT AND ILLUSTRATIONS

Andrea Castellani is founder and legal representative of Cartobaleno Srl, for which he works as director, author, and illustrator. Over the years, he has won numerous awards and accolades and directed many TV series. He also works with many publishers in Italy and around the world as author and illustrator for children's books.

TEXTS

Altea Villa is a content and ghost writer with a PhD in contemporary history. Villa is also a children's book author.

White Star Kids™ is a trademark of White Star s.r.l.

© 2023 White Star s.r.l.
Piazzale Luigi Cadorna, 6
20123 Milan, Italy
www.whitestar.it

Translation: Katherine Kirby
Editing: Abby Young

All rights reserved. No part of this publication may be reproduced, stored or transmitted in any form or by any means without written permission from the publisher.

First printing, August 2023

ISBN 978-88-544-2005-2
1 2 3 4 5 6   27 26 25 24 23

Printed and manufactured in China by Dream Color